WRITING FICTION GOD'S WAY

Remembering
The Creator in creativity

By

Shawn Lamb
Award-winning author of books
for ages 8 through Adult.

Allon Books

www.allonbooks.com

WRITING FICTION GOD'S WAY by Shawn Lamb
Published by Allon Books
209 Hickory Way Court
Antioch, Tennessee 37013
www.allonbooks.com

Cover design by Robert Lamb

International Standard Book Number: 978-0-9891029-4-0

TABLE OF CONTENTS

INTRODUCTION

THE REASON FOR THIS BOOKLET ISN'T to be another resource with tips and instruction for the aspiring writer. No, the reason is to point the hopeful writer to God, and inspire them to use the talent He gave for His glory.

Anyone can teach the mechanics of writing, and there are a myriad of resources dedicated to nothing but instruction on how to write. However, the *heart* of the writer is what is important to God. He not only gives the talent, but also the drive to write. Just like all other aspects of our Christian life, writing should be guided and encouraged through application of God's Word and not simply crafted and manufactured by a man-made writing method.

I studied for 3 years under a well-known Christian writing institute. All materials used came from *secular* resources, and touted as aids for teaching Christians how to crafting a *Godly* story. Yes, I learned a great deal about the *craft* of writing, but the course fell woefully short in the area of Godly application. The lessons soft-pedal the choices Christian writers make in choosing topics and subject matters. It did address Christian principles in *ethics*; however, writing is more than ethics. Life can't be compartmentalized between business writing ethics and private moral behavior and beliefs. There are definite areas of right and wrong in Scripture that should be discussed in "Christian" writing courses.

Once I completed the course, I felt frustrated by the lack of guidance in how to express my faith in writing. Left to my own resources, I did what I had in other aspects of life, and subjected my writing to the application of God's Word.

Sadly, what happened to me is typical of writing courses with an emphasis on making *faith* fit into writing, as if *faith* is an afterthought, and not the primary guiding factor. Creative expression is hammered to the point where self-expression becomes the goal to reach rather than how to please God.

Scripture speaks to the reverse and Christ is **"before all things, and by Him all things**

exist" that He is "**the head of the body"** so that in "**all things He might have preeminence.**" Colossians 1:17-18.

For years I had a blog that deal with writing and faith. I amassed hundreds of followers, and couldn't keep up with the questions on the subject of faith. Most faced the same problem I did, the ability to find great resources on the mechanics, but little to nothing on making it jive with personal faith and beliefs. I tried to answer those questions as best I could on a variety of post dealing with Christian writing and fiction.

At events and book signings, I encountered the same questions from young aspiring writers or parents of such writers: How do I encourage creativity but make it subject to personal faith?

All these factors combined to show me the need for a book to deal with the serious issue of helping Christians understand how faith should guide writing.

In Paul's illustration of the runner in 1 Corinthians 9:24-27, the athlete disciplines his body to run a more effective race. The writer should apply the same Spiritual principle of disciple in crafting a story.

In this booklet, I attempt to answer the issues I resolved by using what I found as the key verse to help me.

Colossians 3:17

> *Whatever you do in word or deed, do all in the name of the Lord Jesus, giving thanks through Him to God the Father.* (NAS)

May you find this booklet a useful companion to writing courses, to help encourage you, or your aspiring young writer to remember *The Creator* in creativity.

CHAPTER 1

The WORD vs. Words

Whatever you do in word or deed, do all in the name of the Lord Jesus, giving thanks through Him to God the Father. Colossians 3:17 (NAS)

The New Testament Greek term *logos* means *something spoken, communication, account.* The English dictionary expands on the Greek by adding *sound or a combination of sounds or its representation in writing or print*. The most well known Bible verses using *logos* are:

John 1:1

In the beginning was the WORD, and the WORD was with God, and the WORD was God.

and **John 1:14**

> *And the WORD became flesh and dwelt among us, and we saw His glory as of the only begotten of the Father, full of grace and truth.* (NAS)

Take a moment to consider these verses since more than a lexicon or definition is implied.

Logos is being used to describe Jesus as the manifestation of God's *communication* with men. How powerful to have Jesus' physical presence and mission summed up in a single *word!* Even when speaking in parables, Jesus used few *words* to convey His message. The same *logos* term is found in Colossians 3:17.

In the New American Standard translation of the New Testament, the term *logos* appears 332 times. When something is used so much, we should pay attention, as there is a significant key point God wants us to know.

Along with being translated *word,* derivatives include: *utterance, report, saying, speech* or other terms for verbal communication. Many verses are warnings about the use of *words.*

Ephesians 4:25

> *… laying aside falsehood, speak truth each one of you …*

Ephesians 4:29

> *… let no unwholesome word proceed from your mouth, but only such a word as is good for edification, so that it will give grace to the hearers.*

Although writers use *written words* to convey a story, the principle is the same. Consider the last part of verse 29.

> *… is good for edification, so that it will give grace to the hearers.*

The Greek term for *edification* means *to build up, to encourage and confirm*. Jesus' parables *confirmed* God's message and gave grace to the hearers.

Writers need to remember that *words*—written or verbal—are powerful tools. While they can bring grace, edification and encouragement, *words* can also bring harm, hurt and destruction.

In James chapter three, the apostle goes to great lengths in discussing the harmful effects of an unbridled tongue—the spoken word. He calls it hypocrisy that with the same source we say words of blessing then cursing others created in the image of God.

In the same way as the tongue, written words of self-expression must be harnessed. Back to Paul's example of a runner:

> **1 Cor. 9:27a**
>
> ... *but I discipline my body to keep it under control* (NAS)

Discipline and control are two sides of the same coin, so to speak. A person who is disciplined will maintain control in all areas of their life, not compartmentalize certain aspects. Sadly, freedom of creative expression is often touted as a virtue thus many Christian authors today don't consider the negative side of what they write. Instead, they place "creative freedom" outside of the discipline called for in Scripture.

Some even go so far as to use Scripture to justify edginess and/or inappropriate subjects in their books. They cite graphic sections of the Bible in portraying sin. This is true, however, a *big distinction must be made between Scripture and fiction.* <u>The Bible was not written for our entertainment</u>!

2 Timothy 3:16

All Scripture is inspired by God and profitable for teaching, for reproof, for correction, for training in righteousness.

2 Peter 1:20-21

But know this first of all, that no prophecy of Scripture is a matter of one's own interpretation, for no prophecy was ever made by the act of human will, but men moved by the Holy Spirit spoke from God.

Scripture is the direct *Word* from God and based upon *His infallible truths*, while fiction is based upon *man's imagination*! Whereas fiction and stories can be a way to convey Godly principles, Scripture should never be used to justify wrong or sinful behavior that an author includes in a book! One should also be careful when claiming a work of fiction to be *inspired* by God.

In 2 Timothy 3:16, the Greek word for *inspired* means *divinely breathed.* The most common word used to refer to the Holy Spirit is *pneuma*, meaning *breath*. This word is where we get the medical terms such as *pneumonia* to speak of lungs, which contains the human breath of life.

The dictionary also defines *inspired* as the *urge or ability to do something creative.* By definition people can be *inspired* to write. However, some Christians take this into the Spiritual realm by claiming God *inspired* them. This is where caution must come into play. By making such a claim, the individual elevates a fictional story on par with God's perfect work.

I've challenged a number of people who have made this *inspired claim.* Most had not realized how the claim sounded and immediately back-pedaled when I asked if they meant their book was equal to God's Holy Word. Some writers were horrified at that thought, really meaning the dictionary's definition. However, after some discussion, understood how what they said came across as boastful.

Yet, a few stubbornly maintained their claim, and YES—even said their book was a supplement to the Bible! They displayed a pride not willing to accept any counter argument based upon Scripture. This also includes willfully ignoring the warning in Revelation 22:18-19 about not taking or adding anything to the Scripture. They refused to acknowledge the fact that *sinful creatures writing for other sinful creatures will always fail, since imperfection cannot write perfection.* Such people should be left for God to deal with.

A writer seeking to honor God will maintain a proper perspective in understanding man is a sinner. Nothing we do is worthy of merit in God's economy, only acts of righteousness matter when one is saved.

In 1 Corinthians 3:12-15, Paul talks about a Christian's work in building upon the foundation of Christ. He contrasts wood, hay and straw against gold, silver and precious stones. In the scheme of things, fiction books are wood, hay and straw. Can they help in conveying truth and uphold Godly principles that lead to gold, silver and precious stones? Yes, when handled properly, but in and of themselves, novels are dross and worthless.

When choosing a subject matter for a fictional story, a Christian writer must keep the eternal in mind. Ask yourself these questions based upon the verses mentioned in this chapter:

- Will what I'm writing build upon Christ' foundation to God's glory?
- How will the story bring grace to readers?

- ♦ How will it edify, encourage and confirm others?

Yes, God created *creativity* to express beauty, thought and to have fun. Writing is fun! It is fulfilling to use a God-given talent as He designed and planned for us. The trick is balancing the fun and creative expression with a motivation and goal that should always point heavenward. By way of a heavenly mindset, one can manage the *words* used to communicate a story, and give account of the characters' lives so as to bring grace and edification to readers.

CHAPTER 2

Fan Fiction Vs. Faith Fiction

WITH THE ADVENT OF THE INTERNET followed by the ease of anyone starting a blog, the rise in *fan fiction* has skyrocketed! *Fan fiction* is exactly what it states: fiction based upon a certain book, movie, and/or comic franchise written by fans. These are usually done for no pay and posted on blogs to be discussed, critiqued and disseminated by fellow fans.

Recently, Amazon signed a contract with a large company representing various media franchises to publish fan fiction on Kindle. The jury is still out on the viability or even good this will do for the industry. However, for this book, *fan fiction* needs to be addressed since many young people are eager to write about their favorite character(s) based upon some established franchise.

Being a *fan* of something isn't necessarily a bad thing, nor is writing *fan fiction* for fun. I've had young fans send me short stories they wrote about *Allon* or pictures of their favorite character(s). A group of 7th grade boys made YouTube video about book 1 and others asked permission to make a stop-motion animated movie. A healthy interest in something is normal, especially for stimulating a child to develop imagination and have fun.

That said, however, being a *fan* can become problematic when a person shows obsessive tendencies relating to topic or subject.

The English word *obsess* comes from the Latin *obsedere* which means *to be harass by an evil spirit.* Other forms can mean *besieged* or *unreasonable compulsion of emotion.* Usually this type of behavior is manifested by a preoccupation or fixation upon an object or person that often defies logic. In Scripture, anything that fits this type of behavior is called *idolatry.*

Giving these definitions isn't to suggest any medical or psychological diagnosis, rather to inform meanings. Still, parents know when a child is becoming *obsessive* with any subject, person or idea by behavioral changes.

Fan fiction can feed an inclination and turn the obsession into *idolatry*. The best way for anyone, young or old, to combat the possibility of *anything* becoming a problem is to be anchored by the Word.

2 Corinthians 10:5

Casting down imaginations, and every high thing that exalts itself against the knowledge of God, and bringing into captivity every thought to the obedience of Christ.

This is a scary verse since writers rely upon imagination and thought to craft a story. But understand that Paul is referring to anything that *exalts*—or *places*—itself above God and Christ. We are made in the likeness of God, thus we have a mind, creativity and imagination. All of which must be guided by God; or as Paul says, "**bringing into captivity every thought to the obedience of Christ.**"

This verse is a good illustration about *balance*. The word *balance* became known as the "B" word in our home, as we kept instilling the concept to our daughter when she was younger. The above verse in Corinthians uses two key words that show an important balance:

KNOWLEDGE

and

IMAGINATIONS.

Knowledge is the Greek word, *gnosis,* which means *clearly expressed, understood, conscience.* Catch the last definition, *conscience.* When we know God's Word, it becomes our *conscience,* our guide. Knowledge can help to maintain a balance to imagination.

The Greek word for *imagination* comes from the root *logos,* yes the same word used in Chapter 1. However, this derivative means *reasoning, computation or thought.* Some translations use the word *speculations.* In this verse, the translation for *knowledge* and *imagination* deal with the mind.

In referring to knowledge the word for *mind* (intellect) is used 95 times in the Bible. Yet the intent goes further than that. In Jewish terms, *heart* is often substituted for mind, since *heart* denotes *behavior,* and appears over 800 times in Scripture. God cares about the heart and character of a person. Remember I said in the introduction, the *heart* of the writer is important to God.

Second Corinthians 10:5 is a good verse to remember in seeking a balance between imagination needed for writing and bringing those thoughts into obedience with God's Word by way of knowledge. This helps to craft stories that bring grace and edification to readers. It will also be easy to write *faith* into fan fiction or, better yet, write an original narrative story of *faith fiction.*

FAITH FICTION

Faith Fiction is where the writer expresses their faith through an original story, and not something based upon another individual's work. Some have suggested that Biblical Fiction featuring people from Scripture is *fan fiction,* but I differ on that viewpoint. People in Scripture are real, factual and relate God's history of events since creation. I place taking a Biblical account and adapting it to prose in the *historical fiction* category.

Faith Fiction can take different forms in various genres, but always with a strong undercurrent of faith, trust and belief in God. Must God be mentioned on every page? Not necessarily. In fact, there is one book in the Bible where God isn't mentioned at all, but

His presence is felt in every word. Can you guess the book?

ESTHER

… if you hadn't guessed it yet.

Not once is God mentioned, yet Esther reads like a novel. It goes in chronological order in almost prose/story-like form. The major theme is *faith.* Although not explicitly mentioned, every action of Mordecai and Esther demonstrates *faith* against life-and-death odds!

The book of *Ruth* is also an example of *faith* in action, though not as dire in consequences as Esther. If you haven't yet, read both of these short books in the Old Testament. They show how *faith* shapes an individual regardless of circumstances.

Examine yourself as a writer. If you are a fan of *fan fiction,* write for amusement and gaining skills as a writer, but strive for originality. Whereas imitation is considered the best form of flattery, utilize the talent God gave you for His purposes in crafting *faith fiction.*

CHAPTER 3

Character Matters

IN CHAPTER 2, I STATED THE JEWISH TERM for *heart* is used over 800 times in Scripture, since it speaks about behavior. Don't miss this—the *heart* in Scripture equals *behavior.* The Western mindset has changed this by making *heart* to mean *feelings.* So we claim whatever we do that involves *feeling* comes from our *heart.* This is actually wrong theology, thus backwards *behavior* on our part.

When addressing issues involving *feelings*, Scripture refers to the *bowels* or the internal organs.

Lamentations 2:11

Mine eyes do fail with tears, my ***bowels*** *are troubled, my liver is poured upon the earth, for the destruction of the daughter of my people…* (KJV)

And in the New Testament:

Philippians 1:8

For God is my record, how greatly I long after you all in the ***bowels*** *of Christ.* (KJV)

The NAS translates the word *bowels* in Lamentations to *my stomach churns.* In Philippians it uses the word *affection* for *bowels*, yet maintains the integrity of the word meaning a *feeling*. Too often authors use the Western mindset as an excuse to express their *heart/feelings.*

Does this mean it's wrong to express one's feelings in writing? Not necessarily. I use writing to vent, but I keep it private to help me process stressful situations—never to see the light of day. However, the current cultural trend is *not* to keep *feelings* private, rather to vent all over the Internet.

There has been a dramatic rise in cyber bullying, blogging and social media venting all in the name of self-expression. People who do so, offer the same excuse to those offended by vitriol: *if you don't like it, too bad, deal with it! I have freedom of speech to say what I want!* Wrong! Others don't need to deal with the selfishness of an individual assaulting anyone for any reason. The one writing needs to deal with an attitude, and doubly so if that person is a Christian, since such actions are totally against Scripture. Remember what was discussed in Chapter 1 dealing with words that hurt verses words that edify.

Jesus dealt directly with this issue in **Matthew 15:17-20**.

> *"Do you not yet understand, that what goes into the mouth goes into the belly and is cast out? But those things which proceed from the mouth come forth from the heart and they defile a man. For out the heart proceeds evil ..."*

There are literally thousands of verses in Scripture dealing with a sinful heart, unrighteousness and lawlessness along with coinciding consequences and curses. When Saul sinned against God multiple times, *the Lord sought out for Himself a man after His own heart. (1 Samuel 13:14)* God sent Samuel to anoint David to replace Saul as King of Israel.

Was David perfect? Far from it! After becoming King, he committed adultery with Bathsheba, murdered her husband, played favorites with his children, was a lousy father and husband. Yet through it all, David's heart remained tender towards God and willingly repented when needed. Due to David's heart and unwavering faith, God made a tremendous promise to this flawed man; David's seed would reign forever! In fact, He would be called the *Son of David* and save His people Israel. He is none other than Jesus, the Christ, Messiah!

From cover to cover, the Bible is populated with flawed, sinful people with one common character trait: a loyal heart for God.

Hebrews 11 is called the "Faith Chapter," as it recounts the lives of these people like a *Who's Who* of Scripture. Each of these individuals failed in many ways, but always looked to God in their weakness and for restoration.

When selecting characters for a story it's easy to pick flawed people since we are all that way.

Romans 3:23

For all have sinned and fall short of the glory of God.

The key is keeping the flaws from being so dominant that the reader loses sight of God. This is a fine line. In Scripture, God doesn't cover the flaws, blemishes or ravages of sin.

However, Scripture isn't written to tempt anyone to sin.

James 1:13

Let no one say when he is tempted, I am being tempted by God, for God cannot be tempted by evil, and He Himself does not tempt anyone.

No, the reason for Scripture is:

2 Timothy 3:16 -17.

All Scripture is inspired by God and profitable for teaching, for reproof, for correction, for training in righteousness. So that the man of God may be adequate, equipped for every good work.

Portraying flawed characters in fiction requires a delicate balance of reality and Godly restraint. Just like in real life, people grow and mature in their faith, actions and behaviors. So should characters in a novel grow and mature during the course of the story. It goes back to *knowing* how God works and what He expects then incorporating those principles into the lives of *imaginary* characters and story.

For younger writers this is difficult since they lack life experiences. To them, I say, don't despair and continue to write.

The basis for *Allon Book 1* was written when I was 16 years old. My historical fiction, *The Huguenot Sword,* was my first completed novel, and also written at age sixteen. Were these stories ready for publication? No, not yet. Like me, the stories matured with age.

Don't be quick to throw away anything you write. *And* don't be in a rush to publish what isn't yet ready. God has His timing for when you and your stories will be ready.

Jeremiah 29:11

> *For I know what plans I have for you, declares the Lord, plans for welfare and not for evil, to give you a future and a hope.*

The same as God has a plan for you and your development, never leave a character hanging in story. Don't suddenly write a personality change. Keep their growth believable. Even heroes (protagonists) should have flaws and weaknesses.

Yet a word of caution when dealing with villains (antagonists), there is no need to go overboard with descriptions of how vile, evil and depraved the character is. Action and dialogue should serve for an adequate portrayal without wallowing in vivid detail. No need to assault the reader with such images. Also giving an antagonist some flaws and showing a softer, more sympathetic side can be intriguing.

Character also matters where the author is concerned because the story reflects upon the their personal beliefs.

When it comes to personal integrity and faith of a writer, it is hard to separate the person from the novel. Why? Because writing is part of the individual, it comes from within. Remember what I said earlier in the chapter about unbridled venting to express one's feelings (heart). An author puts *heart*, soul and a part of him or her self into each character, protagonist and antagonist. Yet he/she must be careful to harness the emotions and words used.

This is why I chose **Colossians 3:17** as the key verse for this booklet.

> *Whatever you do in word or deed, do all in the name of the Lord Jesus, giving thanks through Him to God the Father.* (NAS)

With the Christian life, there should be no compartmentalizing, no division, no distinction between reality and make-believe. The Bible doesn't make a distinction between real-life and fiction, so why should we? Scripture calls us to be consistent in all aspects of our lives.

Just because I put on the hat of a *fiction* writer, doesn't mean I ignore or dismiss my real life relationship to God through Christ! I am still accountable for my actions, and writing about a *fictional* world doesn't change that fact. I don't portray evil or sin for some self-gratification or because I like it and it's fun. I portray these for a reason—to point to God!

Conflict in life is unavoidable, but through God, we can deal with adversity. The conscientious writer will understand the responsibility of differentiating between *venting* and controlled storytelling.

If one looks closely at an author's personal life, you'll find enough evidence of how it influences their novels.

The first thing I do when someone recommends a book is look up the author, not read the back jacket or reviews. Nor does it matter to me if the publisher is a *Christian*. Secular publishing companies now own most of them, and have placed non-Christians in decision-making positions. Sad to say, a *Christian* publisher's logo on a book doesn't necessarily mean the content is Biblical. Therefore, nothing tells me more about what to expect from a book than learning who is the author.

- What do they believe?
- Are they Christian?
- Do they adhere to certain theology?
- What is their background?

Character matters! The personality of the author *will always* influence the lives of those in the novel. If your character and integrity before God is intact, don't compromise it for the sake of writing a *fictional* story. Instead, use your moral fiber to create characters to make a difference in ways that brings the grace of God to those who read the story.

CHAPTER 4

A Certain Point of View

ONE OF THE MOST IMPORTANT ASPECTS of a novel is the Point of View or POV, as it is called in writing terms. This can take several different forms.

The first is the whole POV of the novel, and the second is the POV of the characters—or their personal worldview. The first choice of establishing a novel's POV will affect the character's worldview. Example: is the story set in modern times or another time in history? Characters living in the 17th century won't have the same worldview as those of today. Time and culture play a part in developing a character's personality and thought process.

This world setting is then distilled down the character's POV. The two most common fiction POVs are First Person and Third Person.

First Person is exactly what it states: the story told from a single person's POV, and that is the protagonist.

Although favored by young people today, First Person is the most difficult POV to write. It requires a deft hand and expert handling to carry a full-length novel of 75,000 words or more and not sound drab, narrow-minded or narcissistic by indulging in self-absorbed rambling.

Do my words sound harsh? Being an author, I'm asked to read books, story ideas or manuscripts all the time. I pick and choose what I will read. Sorry to say, some were badly written First Person books by novice self-published authors. They rushed to get their story out and didn't take the time to get help or critiques ahead of time.

As a reader of these books, I felt robbed of a good story. The other characters were so stilted or lambasted by the "main character" they became caricatures and fodder over which the story steamrolled. Thus, as an author, I couldn't see beyond the dreaded "I" and "me" syndrome to what was happening in the story. Those who sought my opinion accepted no amount of counsel, tips or nicely worded suggestions from me.

Instead, the young authors became defensive, and offered the same excuse: First Person gave them an outlet to express themselves. Instead of targeting or harnessing self-expression, self-indulgence was written all over those books. The stories were nothing more than personal *venting*, and made for laborious reads.

First Person is so problematic, I don't recommend young writers attempt this POV until they are well down the road, more familiar with the craft, *and* willing to listen rather than vent.

Yes, I know most courses include lessons in First Person, but these must be handled properly. Again, we go to Scripture for examples of writing First Person the proper way—without self-indulgence.

The Book of Acts is a perfect example of First Person properly handled. Luke states his purpose in Acts 1:1-3 and stays in an omniscient narrative until chapter 16 where it switches to "we" and Luke is included.

However, as a physician, Luke records detailed accounts without any hint of inserting himself or giving an opinion of people or events even though he was an eyewitness. He lets the facts and accounts speak for themselves to those receiving his report.

Another example, in his Gospel and letters, John always refers to himself as *the disciple Jesus loved* in a show of great humility. In Revelation, John does his best to describe the indescribable. Only a few times does he include his reaction of awe, fear or reverence. Mostly, he allows the action and vision to unfold in glorious detail.

The point of storytelling is *not* to inject the author's voice and distract the reader, rather allow people to read the story uninterrupted and let the flow reveal characters, personalities and situation. Let the reader decide what to think about the events and others characters in the story without being told.

Third Person is the best POV for allowing this freedom of storytelling. The author is always present as the narrator, but the situation and characters' worldview shape the story.

A word of caution: if writing historical fiction, the character's worldview should reflect the time in which he or she lived, and not 21st century morals or viewpoints. The basic tenants of Christianity remain unchanged through the centuries, but implementation and some practices were affected by the society of the time.

Again, we look to Scripture to find beautiful stories in Third Person: *Ruth* and *Esther*. We spoke of Esther before, so let's take a closer look at Ruth.

In the book of Ruth, scandalous subjects are dealt with in a delicate and poetic manner. Sleeping at the feet of a man was unthinkable at the time. Ruth was already looked down upon for being a Moabite, but to spend the night beside Boaz was scandalous! The act alone could wreck her virtue beyond repair. Still, Ruth showed no fear and all trust in obeying Naomi.

On his part, Boaz already thought kindly of Ruth when made aware of her kinship to him while gleaning in his fields. That night her obedience and righteous behavior endeared her to Boaz. He took up the mantle of protector and championed her cause. He made a bold, public claim of kinsman redeemer on Ruth's behalf.

The author—God, of course—deals with both Ruth and Boaz individually in portraying their heart and character by way of their words and deeds. They become the focus of the story. Still, the point and purpose of *faith* in God, and their righteous behavior towards Him, is never diminished or overly stated, it is just a fact throughout.

Whichever POV you chose, first examine your heart about motivation as you consider the key verse of **Colossians 3:17**.

> *Whatever you do in word or deed, do all in the name of the Lord Jesus, giving thanks through Him to God the Father.* (NAS)

- Is the choice of POV for *your* self-expression or *His* glory?

- Can you maintain integrity before God if you choose First Person?

Be honest, and be ready to answer for the choices in writing.

CHAPTER 5

Sugary Sweet Or Gritty Reality

A PHRASE HEARD ALL TOO FREQUENTLY in writing is "Be real." What exactly does that mean?

Well, it can mean different things to different people. In some cases, it leads to using Scripture in an effort to rationalize and justify a bad choice.

There is no denying Scripture can be graphic in description, but as stated in Chapter 1, using Scripture to justify fulfilling self-desires in writing is wrong! The examples given in Scripture are for our benefit, not entertainment!

*And fiction **is** entertainment!*

Never lose sight of that.

Can entertainment be fun, educational and helpful? Yes, all of those—*if handled properly.*

Writing a sweet Christian fiction story or adding more gritty elements is walking a fine line. However, we have a guide, and it is called our *conscience.* God gave us a conscience *and* His word to use jointly for making choices.

Psalms 119:11

I have hidden your word in my heart that I might not sin against you.

When speaking on this subject of conscience, some have argued with me about Christian liberty. The argument goes that certain subjects are not problematic to the author, so he or she is free to write what they feel is acceptable to them. This includes graphic scenes and filthy language. After all, cursing and foul language are real and common.

To these authors, anyone who argues against them is not "mature in faith" and just needs to get over it rather than being "ashamed" or even "cowardly" in dealing with these subjects. I know from firsthand experience, and have been dismissed as backwards and old-fashion.

The use of "spiritual maturity" is a straw-man argument. It shows a *heart attitude* (*behavior* in Chapter 3) of disregarding verses in Scripture that address the wrongness of filthy language, while at the same time, using verses to justify their inclusion of such behavior in novels! The hypocrisy of these types of people is mind-boggling.

When cornered, a few explained they *never cuss* in real life, but soldiers and criminals do, so it's fine to have such a character swear. I was in the army back the early 1980s. Such language was *not* commonplace, and certainly not officers to enlisted or men in front of women. Yes, much has changed in society over 30 plus years, but Scripture remains the same concerning *cussing.*

Ephesians 4:29

Let no corrupt communication proceed out of your mouth …

and **Colossians 3:8.**

put them all away: anger, wrath, malice, slander and obscene talk from your mouth.

Real life can be portrayed with creative phrases, like *he spat out an expletive* or *he cursed so much even the cat left the room.* There is no need to assault the readers' sensibilities by using crude language.

As to the argument of Christian *liberty*, are they really free to pursue their own liberty in Christ without responsibility to others or even to God? Not if one truly follows Scripture.

In 1 Corinthians 8, Paul discusses meat offered to idols and deals with the subject of Christian *liberty* in offending a weaker brother. Paul also sums up this same thought in **Galatians 5:13**.

> *For you were called to freedom (liberty), brethren, only do not turn your freedom into an opportunity for the flesh, but through love, serve one another.*

Through books, authors have tremendous influence. Christian authors also have a responsibility before God to consider those who will read their books. What will the impact be upon them? This is where many *Christian* authors fail, by refusing to take into account the repercussion of what they write on weaker and more impressionable minds.

Of course, authors can't control every reaction to our books. All we can do is mitigate them by making wise, God-guiding and honoring choices. It is selfish to dismiss any form of responsibility and just write whatever feels good. A seared conscience makes for seared choices. A tender conscience makes for more delicate choices. There is nothing wrong with refraining from grit to write sweet Christian fiction! There is nothing wrong with a soft, gentle conscience toward God and others!

Unfortunately, too many Christian authors proclaim their *rights* to *write* what they want. In truth, the word *right,* as in relation to able to do as one pleases, only appears in Scripture to describe the negative. Example:

Judges 21:25

Everyone did what was right in their own eyes.

This happened when Israel didn't have a king. Everyone did what they wanted without guidance or conscience. Israel ultimately paid the price of ignoring God with the Babylonian captivity.

Some translations do substitute the word *right* when discussing freedom and liberty in Christ.

But when taking a closer look at the passages, they all give a warning about abusing the freedom with sin.

Our freedom in Christ is from the *bondage* of sin and imprisonment to lawlessness. This gave us the ability to pursue *righteousness* not to claim *rights* to do as we please.

In the New Testament, believers are actually called *doulos* in the Greek. This word means *slave or bondservant.* Translations that use *servant* are downplaying the real term by giving the impression that being a servant is a choice. Yes, we make a *choice* when following Christ, yet, that doesn't negate fulfilling our responsibility to live as witnesses for God, of His righteousness and holiness.

1 Corinthians 6:19-20

> *Do you not know that your body is the temple of the Holy Spirit within you, whom you have from God? You are not your own, for you were bought with a price. So glorify God in your body.*

That price was Christ's precious blood, which He shed on the Cross! Peter goes further in his second epistle to warn against "false teachers and prophets" who will bring destruction by "*denying the Master who bought them*;" again, meaning Christ's blood and sacrifice as the purchased redemption for us!

Clearly Scripture outlines what is acceptable and unacceptable behavior, thoughts and actions for a Christian. Why should those verses, laws and precepts be tossed aside when writing fiction? They shouldn't be.

Some authors, like myself, choose a middle ground between sweet and gritty. What sins Scripture states is wrong I choose not to include in my books in graphic detail. Yet, I deal with hard subjects, as life is hard.

For me, *be real* means portraying life with all its flaws, joy, sorrows, triumphs and tragedies but always keeping God and the eternal in mind for those who read my books. Are my books perfect? Of course not. Remember I said earlier; imperfection can't write perfection. What I strive for is to keep a clear conscience before God when writing.

I don't believe an author who seeks to honor God will be held accountable when someone stumbles without the author's knowledge or intent. God knows the heart of the author.

But, if an author writes knowing full well that the content goes against Scripture and proceeds without regard for the audience, be prepared, for Jesus spoke harshly in **Matthew 18:6** of purposely making someone stumble.

> *But whoever causes one of these little ones who believe in Me to stumble, it would be better for him to have a great millstone fastened around his neck and drowned in the depth of the sea.*

Whichever type of story you choose, sweet or gritty, place before God for His inspection and make your conscience clear. Also keep a tender mind on how others will accept what is written.

CHAPTER 6

Good Vs. Evil

THIS IS A TYPICAL QUESTION WITH Christian fiction in almost any genre: how much evil is too much compared to good? The choice of storyline usually drives the amount of evil that characters face, such as a murder mystery, fantasy or supernatural thriller. This doesn't mean the author needs to wallow in description and inundate the reader with horrid evil.

Life is full of challenges, and evil is a part of this physical world since the Garden. Man is sinful, and the heart deceitfully wicked, thus there is no getting around the facts. Despite this, the main theme of the Bible is *hope! Hope* for a Savior, *hope* for sinners, *hope* for peace with God and *hope* for eternal life.

Since Adam and Eve sinned and brought about the downfall of mankind, God promised *hope* of redemption by way of a Savior. This *hope* has become increasingly difficult to find in the vast majority of Christian fiction.

Christian publishers seem more concerned with the edgier stories. They want authors to push the envelope and take the reader to places "Christian" fiction has never gone before. This has led to a dramatic rise in Christian Speculative fiction and "Christian" fiction imitating the world's trend with the introduction of inappropriate material.

In 2009, a book published by Broadman & Holman, the publishing arm of the Southern Baptist Convention, won the prestigious *Christy Award* for best Christian fiction. The title of the book: *MEMOIRS of a DEMON* by Tosca Lee.

In numerous interviews, Lee declared her favorite author is Anne Rice, and specifically Rice's book *Interview with a Vampire!* In all the interviews, I've read and listened to, Lee never addresses the fact that Rice was raised Catholic and turned *atheist* for the expressed purpose of writing sensual books. In fact, Rice proudly stands by her denunciation of anything Christian! Still, Lee continues to model her writing after Rice. This gives insight into the subject matter of her books, as well as Lee's personal beliefs regarding Christianity.

In 2011, Ted Dekker paired with Tosca Lee to write *FORBIDDEN*, the first in a mortal trilogy about *zombies.* The publisher is Hachette Books, which is owned by Time Warner. Some places will say *Faithwords*, which is a "religious" imprint of Hachette. The same as Thomas Nelson and Zondervan are now "religious" imprints of Harper Collins.

As I stated in an early chapter, these companies are not owned or run by Christians. They may employ some Christians, but the vast majority of publishing decisions are not based upon Scripture.

The market dictates the trends in fiction and not Biblical principle. To counteract or even hide this fact, publishers will place a false face on the book by giving it a *Christian* spin.

For example:

When *Forbidden* was released, Hachette put out a press summary of the book stating the *magic vial of blood* that makes people come alive from their *zombie* state to experience feelings, which can turn them either good or *evil*, is a symbol of *Christ's blood!* Suddenly, a gory book about zombies becomes "Christian" in nature due to this claim and not anything Biblical.

There is major theological problem here—the atoning work of Christ's blood does *not* turn anyone to evil!

Such a bold claim by the publisher regarding Christ's *real* sacrifice being equal to a *fictional blood* that turns people to evil is dangerous! It undermines the saving work of the Christ by using Him as a *marketing tool*.

These marketing strategies are not by accident. In June 2011, the advisory committee to the Department of Homeland Security submitted a report that contains disturbing trends every American should be aware of. They call this *Resilience Preparedness.* This document is available for viewing on the DHS website, and specifically outlines tactics dealing with the media and kids on pages 21 and 22.

On page 21, the report says this is what DHS needs to launch:

> *"A robust television, print, and social media advertising campaign … Television shows and movies have long been used to foster* NEW *behavioral norms …* SO *certain resilience behaviors could be similar modeled."* (Emphasis added)

Take note of the admission of the government using the media to *influence* people and make *behavioral* modifications.

Along with this effort, the report outlines a *parallel* process of using television, print and social media:

> *"to go into schools to "inculcate a renewed sense and mindset of personal responsibility."*

Responsibility to whom, you might ask? The answer is in the definition given in the report about *resilience:*

> *"Ability of systems, infrastructures, government, business and citizenry to resist, absorb, recover from, or adapt to an adverse occurrence that may cause harm, destruction, or loss of national significance."*

That's right, the DHS is to use all forms of media to make people unified for the sake of *national significance.*

What does that mean?

Anything the government deems worthy—or what they consider unworthy that would interfere with such an effort.

These marketing campaigns are not without purpose, nor are the inclusion of inappropriate subject matters into books.

According to the DHS, all this is to make the population believe alternative lifestyles are normal, and to blunt the impact of Christians on society by covertly inserting topics into *fiction* that is contrary to Scripture. After all, books are just make-believe. The problem is if one believes a lie long enough, it becomes truth.

Christian fiction *is* mimicking the world's trend. More disappointing is the rising numbers of Christians agreeing with the so-called theology being put forth in these stories!

Walk the aisles of a Christian bookstore and discover fiction books about vampires, evil twins called "doppelgangers," ghosts, witches and paranormal romance dealing with inappropriate relationships between people, angels or demons. Many of these books are being aimed at kids!

For all intents and purposes, this trend has succeeded in removing Biblical values from "Christian" fiction. Discernment among Christian readers is almost non-existent, as told by singing the praises of such authors as Lee and Dekker, and convincing others to read them.

This acceptance does not mean every Christian writer must compromise! In fact, just the opposite, they must stand firm. There is more at risk than book sales. *God's honor is at stake!*

The gap between authors who wish to stay true to Godly virtue and those pursuing rougher issues is so vast they are now at opposite ends of the spectrum, but both continue to use the "Christian" label.

An author must make tough choices when it comes to portraying good and evil. This is at the heart of many verses in Scripture in dealing with sin and righteousness. Perhaps none is as direct in stating the fact as this verse:

James 4:4

Friendship with the world is enmity with God!

Jesus said you cannot serve two masters. Although He was speaking of money, the principle is the same. A Christian writer cannot please God and serve the world by catering to its lusts!

We are called to be different, separate, a *royal priesthood* (1 Peter 2:9). We are God's representatives on earth, and witnesses for Christ. We are to be in the world but not of the world. (Romans 12:1-2 and John 15:19-20) Our witness for Christ becomes null and void if we chose to gain favor from men rather than God.

Remember, writing is a talent given to you by God to use for His purposes, not worldly gain or recognition. Including too much evil, places the focus on the Enemy, who does not deserve such attention. Choose wisely the balance between the portrayal of good and evil.

A way to accomplish this is by maintaining a theme of *hope* throughout the book. This way, you as the author, will be able to keep God in the forefront of your mind, thus in the story. That will translate to the reader.

Joshua 24:15

"Choose this day whom you will serve … But for me and my house, we will serve the Lord." (NAS)

Are you willing to take Joshua's challenge to the Israelites when thinking of your writing in relationship to portraying good and evil? Will you mimic worldly trends or stay true to Biblical principles?

Colossians 3:17

Whatever you do in word or deed, do all in the name of the Lord Jesus, giving thanks through Him to God the Father. (NAS)

CHAPTER 7

Miraculous or Ordinary

THIS CHAPTER MAY SOUND LIKE A REPEAT of the previous chapter dealing with Good vs. Evil, and there is some overlap. However, it comes from a question I hear a lot because I write fantasy. So, I'm going to take some time to explain what I believe is the difference between *magic* and *supernatural,* and being balanced by the *ordinary.*

When I was young, *magic* was considered tricks or slight of hand, and nothing dangerous or evil. That is not the true definition of *magic,* nor the proper root of where it comes from. The word itself means *to move or influence in a mysterious way.*

Throughout history *magic* and *superstition* were used interchangeably since unlearned people couldn't explain natural phenomena of weather, stars, comets or such. They did acknowledge deities, supernatural beings beyond the realm of humankind. Weather and nature phenomena excluded, the majority of *magic* and *supernatural* occurred by demonic forces to ensnare people.

This "magic" sometimes involved human agents, witches and warlocks. Of course, these people are *always* associated with the enemy and darkness.

Stories that attempt to introduce *white magic* as good and beneficial by attributing it to God are in direct violation of Scripture in regards to witchcraft! *All uses of magic violate Scripture, whether in reality or fiction!*

In no uncertain terms, these Bible verses condemn witches and witchcraft:

- Exodus 22:18
- Deuteronomy 18:10
- 1 Samuel 15:23
- 2 Chronicles 33:6
- 2 Kings 9:22
- Micah 5:12
- Nahum 3:4

- Galatians 5:20

These statements are strongly worded, with no ambiguity, for any misunderstanding. The Exodus verse says *you shall not suffer a witch to live!* While Deuteronomy gives a specific list of offensive behavior that is *not to be found among you* including, burning children as an offering, divinations, fortunetellers, interprets omens, sorcerer, charmer, medium, necromancer or séances.

People who refuse to adhere to the prohibition or minimize these verses place themselves in the category of *rebellion* against the authority of God's Word.

Here is what **1 Samuel 15:23** says about rebellion:

> *For rebellion is as the sin of witchcraft* …

The sin is compounded when books like Harry Potter are used to preach sermons and teach Sunday School classes claiming the characters are representations of Christ and Christian principles.

Do you think I exaggerate? Go on the Internet and Google *Harry Potter as a Christ-like figure* and read how many so-called *theologians* espouse this principle!

People argue from both sides of whether J.K. Rowling is a *Christian* or a *Wiccan.* Rowling has further muddied the waters about her personal religious views by condemning Christianity yet claiming to belong to the Church of Scotland. She readily admits to the inclusion of Pagan rites and rituals while stating in the same breath that such practices are equal with Christian tenets! In short, she tries to play both sides against the middle with platitudes.

However, what people believe or say is of no consequence when Scripture is clear on an issue. In Matthew 11:22-32, Jesus states what *HE* thinks of those likening the power of God to Satan when the Jewish leaders accused Him of casting out demons by the power of the *prince* of demons.

> *'Every kingdom divided against itself is laid waste, and no city or house divided against itself will stand. If Satan cast out Satan, he is divided against himself. How then will his kingdom stand?"*

Then *Jesus* issues a dire warning:

> *'Therefore I tell you, every sin and blasphemy will be forgiven people, but the blasphemy against the Spirit will not be forgiven … either in this age or in the age to come."*

Magic *does not* exist, but supernatural beings *do* exist and occupy space around us. From cover to cover, the Bible is filled with supernatural events, both direct intervention by God or His angels.

Angels appear 108 times in the Old Testament and 165 times in the New Testament! The word *devil* or *devils* appears 105 times in Scripture. Yes, angels and fallen angels are very active. By the sheer volume of their involvement in worldly affairs, there is no denying they exist.

Portraying the *supernatural* must be done with great care. Whenever angels appear in Scripture, it is always to do the will of God! This can be for an individual's good or corporate judgment in carrying out God's punishment. They do not act on their own, and work within parameters. Even Satan is shown seeking permission from God to act against Job.

In the *Allon* series, a talisman serves as a visual aid to make a connection between the Shadow Warriors—evil immortals—and those dabbling in the Dark Way. Never does any power originate from the mortals, Latham or Musetta. I make a direct link beyond those who might be called *witch* or *warlock* to the real power—the supernatural beings.

By way of Guardians and Shadow Warriors, mighty, immortal, yet created beings, I bring to life the invisible aspect of spiritual warfare. This is where the *supernatural* comes into play within my stories. Still, they are not direct representations of angles and demons, merely stereotypes for conveying the battle.

One of the most important aspects to writing about the supernatural is to balance it with *ordinary* aspects of the story. The every day struggles of daily life makes the characters more real. This keeps believability from being discredited by continual and/or sudden unexplained occurrences.

A story solely based on the *fantastical* can become wearisome to readers, as they seek to figure how things fit together. To better associate with the world, characters and situations, readers need something to grab onto that can serve as an anchor.

Establish limitations of the supernatural early in the story then remain consistent. This sets up for a more dramatic impact when something supernatural does happen and readers can feel from the protagonist.

Also, don't use the supernatural to get the hero out of a jam or at a crossroads where the character must act or make a choice. The supernatural should be an element of the story, but not the driving force that changes the characters. With human nature, it is the internal, emotional struggle that makes a person.

Just like with the other choices concerning the story, subject the use of the supernatural to guidance of Scripture.

CHAPTER 8

To Romance or Not to Romance

THIS QUESTION CAN BE AS DIFFICULT to handle as other aspects, and can quickly get out of control if not harnessed at the beginning. Even in "Christian" Romance, the boundaries are being pushed into inappropriate areas.

There is a group on Facebook where "Christian" authors are lobbying readers to aid in their effort of convincing publishers to include explicit sex scenes between married characters! Their reason: sex is in Scripture. Adam *knew* Eve and Abraham *knew* Sarah. So, it's natural, and Christians shouldn't be ashamed of writing about it or reading it.

Really?

What part of *thou shalt not commit adultery* do they not understand? Or in Deuteronomy where God talks about not uncovering the nakedness of others for pleasure? Or the countless verses warnings about the consequences of sexual temptation, fornication and sin?

Inevitably, a few on this Facebook page brought up the *Song of Solomon* to argue their point. Yes, God's design the relationship between husband and wife as a wonderful aspect of marriage. But again, the *Song of Solomon* was *not* written to entice people to sin!

Scripture is *clear* on the topic of temptation and where the fault lies.

James 1:13-14

> *Let no one say when he is tempted, I am being tempted by God, for God cannot be tempted by evil, and He Himself does not tempt anyone. But every man is tempted when he is drawn away of his own lust, and enticed. Then when lust has conceived, it brings forth sin; and sin, when it is finished, brings forth death.*

By God's design, romance and human relations is between a man and woman, and strictly monitored according to the laws and precepts God established. The book of Ruth is a beautiful picture of *romance* with piety, honor and virtue on the part of both Ruth and Boaz.

By the comments on this Facebook page, it's obvious the motive of these "Christian" authors is not pure, undefiled or innocent. They want to bring the world's view of *romance* into the Christian arena.

Even sadder, is the fact readers post responses on the page agreeing to aid these authors to profligate this sexual sin by rationalizing the behavior for the sake of more "romance" in Christian fiction.

The word *rationalize* means *to make comfortable, self-satisfying decisions based upon incorrect behavior.* They are obviously ignoring the clear statement of Jesus in Matthew 18:5-7:

> *Whoever receives one such child in my name receives Me, but whoever causes one of these little ones who believes in Me to sin, it would be better for him to have a great millstone fastened around his neck and to be drowned in the depth of the sea. Woe to the world for temptations to sin! For it is necessary that*

> *temptations come, but woe to the one by whom the temptation comes!* (NAS)

Yes, I used this verse earlier in Chapter 5 and it bears repeating in this context as well since Jesus isn't meaning the natural trials and temptations of life that happen to help perfect our faith. This passage is specifically speaking of the consequences of *willfully tempting another believer to sin!* Some translations use the word *stumble,* but *sin* is a more correct interpretation of the Greek word.

I know I might be sounding like a broken record by now, but like the other aspects discussed in previous chapters, Scripture must guide the writing of *romance.*

In reality, there is no aspect of a fiction book that should fall outside the guidance of Scripture. No character, scene or storyline where God is not considered.

When our daughter was young, the letters WWJD were popular. The letters stand for *What Would Jesus Do* and were found on t-shirts, Bible covers, cups, mugs, and all manner of merchandise. Everywhere one went WWJD was seen.

The trend has faded now; but if it helps, think of WWJD when writing a story. Consider Jesus your target audience with others being given access, but your writing falls under His scrutiny. How will that thought affect your choices when it comes to *romance*?

1 Corinthians 6:15-18

Do you not know that your bodies are members of Christ? Shall I then take a member of Christ and make them members of a prostitute? Never! Or do you not know that he who is joined to a prostitute is one body with her? … he who is joined to the Lord becomes one spirit with Him. <u>Flee from sexual immorality!</u>

Jesus is with you in all you do.

CHAPTER 9

Compromise to Witness?

I TOUCHED A BIT UPON THIS SUBJECT IN Chapter 5 when addressing "Gritty Reality," but let's dig a little deeper into this prevalent excuse.

When those defending their choice of vividly portraying *gritty reality* speak about spiritual maturity, they are describing the world's standards of maturity not Biblical Standards. The world draws a line between *mature adults* and *immature adults* in terms of tolerance of inappropriate subject matters. If you can't take cussing and reading sex, then you are *immature* and need to grow up. This, of course is the reverse of Scripture. Growing up according to Scripture is becoming more Christ-like, not more worldly.

Romans 12:1-2

I appeal to you therefore, brothers, by the mercies of God, to present your bodies a living sacrifice, holy and acceptable to God, which is your spiritual service. Do not be conformed to this world, but be transformed by the renewal of your mind, that by testing you may discern what is the will of God, what is good and acceptable and perfect. (ESV)

Note the phrase *spiritual service* is used in reference to God, not to worldly reality. Paul outlines the qualifications of elders and deacons:

1 Timothy 3:2-8

Therefore an overseer must be above reproach, the husband of one wife, sober-minded, self-controlled, respectable, hospitable, able to teach, not a drunkard, not violent but gentle, not quarrelsome, not a lover of money. He must manage his own household well, with all dignity keeping his children submissive. For if someone does not know how to manage his own household, how will he care for God's church? …

> Vs. 8: *Deacons likewise must be dignified, not double-tongued …*

For the rest of the believers Paul states it clearly in 1 Corinthians 11:1.

> *Be imitators of me, as I am of Christ.*

Peter adds to Paul's encouragement.

2 Peter 1:5-8

> *For this very reason, make every effort to supplement your faith with virtue, and virtue with knowledge, and knowledge with self-control, and self-control with steadfastness, and steadfastness with godliness, and godliness with brotherly affection, and brotherly affection with love. For if these qualities are yours and are increasing, they keep you from being ineffective or unfruitful …*

Understanding the difference between the worldly view of *maturity* and true Biblical maturity is key to not being swept up in the prevalent argument of *compromise in order to witness.* Granted there are some authors who genuinely feel they must make some compromises to expose otherwise non-Christians to read their books in *hope* of winning them to Christ.

Good intentions aside, how will that help? How is misrepresenting Christ or Biblical principles in a *fiction* book a good witnessing tool? What happens when that non-Christian reader discovers the *real* doctrine prohibiting fornication, but it was included in a "Christian" novel? A bait-and-switch tactic for witnessing?

Scripture is very specific when it comes to what is and isn't sin. There are no grey areas where evil and good are concerned. In fact, the word *compromise* isn't found in the Bible.

Those people I used as examples in Chapter 5, who claim they never cuss but have no problem letting their character(s) do so, would fall into the category Paul described in Timothy about being *double-tongued.*

The Greek word means to *say something different each time.* In today's vernacular, it is *double-talk*, saying one thing while doing something else.

James used a variation of the same Greek term in his epistle: "… *he is a double-minded man, unstable in all his ways.*" (1:8) and *"Cleanse your hand, you sinners, and purify your heart, you double-minded."* (4:8)

Scripture upon Scripture speaks to growing in grace and the knowledge of Christ while being cleansed from the world. Jesus was very specific when giving what has become known as "The Great Commission."

Matthew 28:19

Go therefore and make disciples of all nations, baptizing them in the name of the Father and of the Son and of the Holy Spirit, teaching them to observe all that I have commanded you.

Witnessing to the world has very defined parameters: *teaching* and *observe. Teaching* is obvious in meaning. *Observe* is the Greek word for *keep, guard or apply*. It is a military term so it implies a strict diligence. This brings us full circle to what I began the chapter with—being examples for others in what the Bible describes as *spiritual maturity*.

Another word to describe those who say their real-life personal beliefs are separate from their fiction is *hypocrite.* The Greek word means *to play-act, to pretend.* In ancient Greece, actors were called *hypocrites,* as they often wore masks when *pretending* to be someone else.

Now, some of you might be thinking about what Paul said in 1 Corinthians 9:22,

> *I have become all things to all people that by all means I might save some.*

Paul wasn't talking about compromising Godly principles rather he was speaking in a cultural context. He just spent the previous chapters discussing meat offered to idols and offending a weaker brother by eating. Sitting to eat kosher food with a Jew or non-kosher food with a Gentile didn't compromise his belief in Christ. Also, he was speaking to fellow believers about how to treat other weaker-minded fellow believers in Christ.

NEVER did Paul suggest in any of his epistles that a believer compromise the mandates of Scripture to win an unbeliever for Christ. He didn't tell them to go to the temple of Diana and engage a prostitute in order to win her soul for Christ. He never encouraged a fellow believer to talk like a *heathen* with filthy language in order to win that soul for Christ.

Our God-given duty to witness to the world is the fact that Christ died for our sins to reconcile hopeless humanity to God. Yes, some Christians feel compelled to write in hopes of reaching the lost, and that's noble and good—if done correctly and according to Biblical principles. Skewing the message to suit the audience never works.

Jesus didn't change His message even when many considered it offensive, for it showed them that their best wasn't good enough and exposed their sin for what it was.

Don't fall for the term *politically correct,* which is bandied about as a noble mindset to aspire to so as not to offend. Jesus didn't, and He was best storyteller who ever lived. The same set of Biblical standards one claims to guide their life should also be evident in their writing.

CHAPTER 10

Ultimate Purpose

THE WESTMINSTER SHORTER CATECHISM starts off with this question:
What is the chief end of man?

The response: *Man's chief end is to glorify God and to enjoy Him forever.*

In the same respect a Christian author should ask: *What is the chief reason for writing a book?*

Hopefully, the answer will be: *To glorify God and enjoy Him in all I do.*

In **1 Corinthians 9:24-27**, the illustration of a runner is so rich with imagery and tremendous application to all aspects of a Christian's life that an entire book could be written just on this passage. I'll try to contain myself to points germane to a writer.

Verse 24 starts out with a rhetorical question.

> *Do you not know that in a race all runners run, but only one receives the prize?* (EVS)

The obvious answer is *yes* since that is common knowledge. Paul then encourages us to run the race to obtain the prize, which according to the passage, is our higher calling in Christ by maturing in our faith.

Verse 25 contains key words of how the athlete accomplishes his task: by way of *self-control,* or *temperate* in other translations. For this verse I like the New King James translation, which says,

> *And every man that strives for <u>mastery</u> is temperate in all things.*

The Greek word *mastery* shows a conquering of a task or a skill, while the word *strive* indicates a struggle. Athletes endure long hours of difficult training over years, decades sometimes, simply to win a medal—or in Paul's time, a laurel wreath.

People can understand and accept that imagery when it comes to sports. Unfortunately, that *striving to master* is often thrown out the window when it comes to the creative arts. For many the idea of self-expression is paramount and shouldn't be subjected or confined by rules.

Really? Says who?

Certainly not Scripture! Remember the key verse for this booklet:

Colossians 3:17

Whatever you do in word or deed, do all in the name of the Lord Jesus, giving thanks through Him to God the Father. (NAS)

Back in 1 Corinthians 9, Paul states in verses 26 -27:

So I do not run aimlessly; do not box as one beating the air. But I discipline my body and keep it under control lest after preaching to others I myself should be disqualified.

The key words are *discipline*, *under control* and *disqualified.* A writer must be *disciplined*, not just in time spent writing, but also in subject matter and words used to craft a story. Self-expression should be kept *under control* like any other part of a Christian's life.

By not adhering to Godly principles in crafting a fiction story, the writer risks being *disqualified.* This might not happen by worldly standards, rather in being a useful servant of God for His glory and honor.

- How can one be a proper witness for Him if they don't <u>discipline</u> what and how they write?

- How can one <u>qualify</u> as a true representative of a royal priesthood if what they write doesn't match what they claim to believe?

- How can one be a role model if they live a life that is not under God's <u>control</u>?

Being in the Body of Christ we are given Spiritual gifts to use for the edification of the Body and aiding fellow believers in Christ.

Talents are another blessing from God. Shouldn't they fall under the control of God for His purposes? Of course! So why do many Christians want to create a divide between spiritual gifts and God-given talents? One doesn't have to look far to answer that question.

Creating an artificial division allows them to compartmentalize their lives and thus rationalize desires, such as the example I gave in the last chapter dealing with the Facebook group.

Are some people so foolish as to truly believe God doesn't see their heart when it comes to choices?

1 Samuel 16:7

For man looks on the outward appearance, but the Lord looks at the heart.

No one can fool God. Even Jesus tells us in Matthew 7:17-18 & 20

Even so, every good tree brings forth good fruit, but a corrupt tree brings forth evil fruit. A good tree cannot bring forth evil fruit; neither can a corrupt tree bring forth good fruit … By their fruit you shall know them.

When it comes to writing, what fruit do you want to be known by?

Do not compartmentalize your life or rationalize choices, for you will not fool God.

Ephesians 6:6

not with eye-service, as men pleasers, but as the servants of Christ, doing the will of God from the heart.

With your writing, *whom* do you want to please?

These are hard questions, but well worth answering before even sitting down to write the first draft of a story. If you allow God and His Word to guide you in choices you make for your writing, it can be a most rewarding experience.

1 Peter 5:6.

Humble yourself under the mighty hand of God, that He may exalt you in good time.

Other Books by Shawn Lamb

Young Adult Fantasy Fiction

ALLON ~ BOOK 1

Published by Creation House, a division of Charisma Media

Published by Allon Books

ALLON ~ BOOK 2 ~ INSURRECTION
ALLON ~ BOOK 3 ~ HEIR APPARENT
ALLON ~ BOOK 4 ~ A QUESTION OF SOVEREIGNTY
ALLON ~ BOOK 5 ~ GAUNTLET
ALLON ~ BOOK 6 ~ DILEMMA
ALLON ~ BOOK 7 ~ DANGEROUS DECEPTION
ALLON ~ BOOK 8 ~ DIVIDED
ALLON ~ BOOK 9 ~ IN PLAIN SIGHT
PARENT STUDY GUIDE FOR ALLON ~ BOOKS 1-4
THE ACTIVITY BOOK OF ALLON

For Young Readers – ages 8-10
Allon ~ The King's Children series

NECIE AND THE APPLES
TRISTINE'S DORGIRITH ADVENTURE
NIGEL'S BROKEN PROMISE

Historical Fiction

GLENCOE
THE HUGUENOT SWORD

www.ingramcontent.com/pod-product-compliance
Lightning Source LLC
LaVergne TN
LVHW010941110826
845149LV00013B/2709

9780989102940